MW00696445

The Perfect Little Project Management Toolkit

PALLAS

THE PERFECT
LITTLE PROJECT
MANAGEMENT

TOOLKIT

The ONLY Tools You Need To Start
Managing SUCCESSFUL Project
Teams, TODAY!!!

BY: JACKSON PALLAS

Copyright © 2019 by JD PALLAS Consulting, LLC. All Rights Reserved.

All rights reserved. No part of this publication may be reproduced, distributed, or transmitted in any form or by any means, including photocopying, recording, or other electronic or mechanical methods, without the prior written permission of the publisher, except in the case of brief quotations embodied in critical reviews and certain other noncommercial uses permitted by copyright law.

10 9 8 7 6 5 4 3 2 1

Licensing/permission requests, may be submitted to the publisher at:

JD PALLAS Consulting, LLC
199 14th Street NE
Atlanta, GA 30309
1.917.983.7933
info@jdpallasconsulting.com

Bulk Order Information:

Special discounts are available on quantity purchases by corporations, associations, bookstores, wholesalers, and others. For details, contact the publisher, using the information provided above.

Printed in the USA.

© 2019 | JD PALLAS Consulting | All Rights Reserved

WHAT IS THE POINT OF THIS BOOK?

To be honest, I chose to put together this guidebook simply because nothing like it has ever existed. Ever.

Many years ago, when I was a young college student searching for something that could provide me with a quick, simple explanation on how to effectively manage any team-based project...I came up empty handed.

What I did find, however was an overwhelming saturation of two other book types...

© 2019 | JD PALLAS Consulting.| All Rights Reserved

1. Dense, academic-style textbooks, written by subject matter experts who spoke to the general discipline of project management as a profession.

2. Concept-based, self-help books that spoke to broader themes about what it takes to be an effective team manager (i.e., organization, hard work, persistence, blah, blah, blah).

Now, don't get me wrong, both of those book types definitely serve their purpose – particularly for those looking to embark on a full-fledged professional career in this space.

© 2019 | JD PALLAS Consulting | All Rights Reserved

However, none of that stuff was helpful to me at the time.

At the end of the day, I just wanted someone to tell me exactly what to do and how to do it.

So, that's precisely what this is. And, as a matter of fact, from the very moment you have finished reading through this book, you will be fully equipped with all of the fundamental know-how you would need to manage the vast majority of team-based projects.

Period.

© 2019 | JD PALLAS Consulting | All Rights Reserved

INTRO

Pain Points..3

Value...11

Setup..13

Process..19

TOOLKIT

Plan...29

Protocol...43

Reporting...51

Agenda..63

Meeting..73

Minutes..87

CONCLUSION

Resolution.................................101

Bottom Line.............................103

Next Steps...............................106

Final Thought..........................109

APPENDIX

Glossary...................................115

Extras.......................................125

For additional tips and information, please visit: www.littlepmtoolkit.com

© 2019 | JD PALLAS Consulting | All Rights Reserved

INTRO

Know this…

EVERY SINGLE HUMAN who has ever managed **any** team of **any** kind in an attempt to achieve **any** common goal (large or small) has very likely experienced one or more of these **10 most frequent team management challenges**:

X Team members don't do what they are supposed to do.

X Team meetings are horribly unproductive, because either:
- team members arrive unprepared, or
- discussion focus veers away from the actual work that needs to get done

© 2019 | JD PALLAS Consulting | All Rights Reserved

✘ There is a difference of opinion about who said what, and it had an effect on the work that needed to get done.

✘ Information is siloed. Everyone doesn't know everything that's being worked on by each of the other team members.

✘ No one knows how well the overall project is really going, because no one knows whether or not every single thing that needs to get done will actually get done on time and at cost.

✘ Things that "need to get done" keep coming up, long after the project is kicked off.

© 2019 | JD PALLAS Consulting | All Rights Reserved

X Team members don't realize the impact their individual work has on other team members and/or overall team success.

X Individual team members become exhausted with and/or disengaged from project team interactions.

X It is frustrating to create working documentation, because of the sheer quantity of information that needs to be organized.

X You (the team leader) want to leverage a document you saw somewhere before to help with your new project, but you can't seem to find it.

As a matter of fact, **RIGHT NOW**… somewhere in the world…somebody is **struuuuggling**!

It could be a C-suite executive scrambling to ensure that all of his or her managers are prepared for a post-merger integration.

It could be an event planner trying to manage a number of third-party vendors, simultaneously.

It could be a PTA president working to organize a school fundraiser.

It could be an ambitious college student failing to get their not-so-ambitious peers to contribute to a major group project.

© 2019 | JD PALLAS Consulting | All Rights Reserved

Who knows? But nevertheless, **ALL of these individuals, whether they realize it or not, are actually operating as a project manager**.

The problem is (especially if they don't realize this fact), they may not have undertaken this effort as would a professional project manager.

And, had they done so, odds are that their life would be going a LOT smoother right now.

Sigh If only there was a user-friendly book of basic tools that could easily help **anyone** do exactly what real project managers do to get teams from Point A to Point B.

© 2019 | JD PALLAS Consulting | All Rights Reserved

Enter *The Perfect LITTLE Project Management Toolkit*

This toolkit is the answer to that frequently troubling question, "How do I get my team to get all this stuff done as effectively and efficiently as possible?"

Sidebar – if you have never experienced any one of the aforementioned pain points, please give me a call directly... because I would love to meet a real unicorn.

Let me let you in on a little secret…
You don't need to know everything about project management to manage projects successfully.

All you really need is a set of simple instructions to a few basic project management tools – which happen to be so user friendly they can help you get the job done right, from day one.

Thus, *The Perfect LITTLE Project Management Toolkit* was intentionally designed to be a quick reference guide, for readers ages 12 to 112, who are leading ANY kind of project team.

© 2019 | JD PALLAS Consulting | All Rights Reserved

That said, please note that this book is **not** a capture of all of the tools and resources used by professional project managers.

It is simply a collection of what many, **many** project management experts deem to be the most critical, most versatile resources that ANYONE managing a project can (and should) make use of.

The tools consolidated in this text are derived from the very best project management practices, which have been proven to be successful time and time again, regardless of company size, industry, and location.

© 2019 | JD PALLAS Consulting | All Rights Reserved

Think of this toolkit like a quick reference guide that holds just as much information as an academic textbook but (literally) fits inside of your pocket.

This book has been deliberately structured and formatted so that readers can instantly access whatever information they might be looking for at any given time.

The following page illustrates precisely how the information is organized throughout the entire book.

[*INFORMATION CATEGORY*]

The most critical points of information about each tool have been organized as follows:

1. Textbook Talk (academic terms)
2. Simple Breakdown (layman's terms)
3. Basic Benefits
4. Illustration & Template Link
5. Best Practices

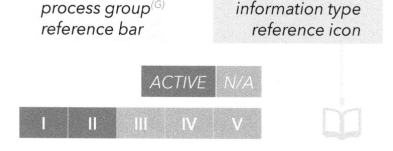

process group(G)
reference bar

information type
reference icon

ACTIVE N/A

| I | II | III | IV | V |

[*INFORMATION CATEGORY*]

The most critical points of information about each tool have been organized as follows:

 ## TEXTBOOK TALK

This category provides a **standard academic and/or professional explanation**, defining what the tool is and the reason for its use.

SIMPLE BREAKDOWN

This category provides an **extremely straightforward explanation**, defining what the tool is and the reason for its use.

[*INFORMATION CATEGORY*]

The most critical points of information about each tool have been organized as follows:

 BASIC BENEFITS

This category provides a **simple summary of the value** that can be realized from the proper use of each tool.

 ILLUSTRATION & TEMPLATE

This category provides a **real-world** example of the actual end-product –and– a link to a free downloadable template.

© 2019 | JD PALLAS Consulting | All Rights Reserved

[*INFORMATION CATEGORY*]

The most critical points of information about each tool have been organized as follows:

 BEST PRACTICES

This category provides a **bulleted list of expert-level habits** that have consistently been proven to help set project managers up for success.

© 2019 | JD PALLAS Consulting | All Rights Reserved　　17

OVERVIEW

The Project Management Body of Knowledge (PMBOK(G)) is essentially the foremost publication on the planet explaining project management as a professional discipline.

The PMBOK Guide thoroughly defines each of the **five process groups** that *all* successful projects must go through, in some way.

Often times, these process groups operate much like work phases, serving as a step-by-step pathway that guides you from point A to point B.

© 2019 | JD PALLAS Consulting | All Rights Reserved

OVERVIEW (continued)

The duration of these process groups varies widely based on need (i.e., it could take five minutes, five days, five weeks, etc.). And, depending on the approach and/or findings of the effort, any one of the process groups may need to be revisited at some point before the project can actually be completed.

Throughout this book, you will notice a graphic bar in the bottom left corner of every project tool description page. This reference bar is meant to serve as a legend, by which you can quickly identify the process groups in which the tool is primarily used.

OVERVIEW (continued)

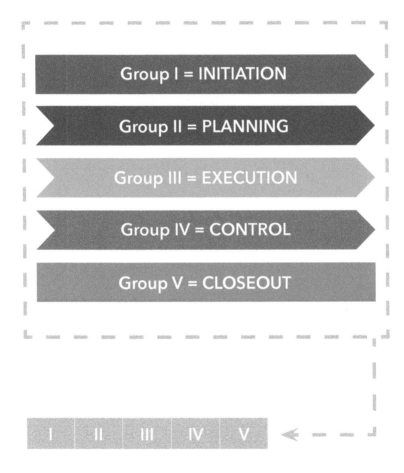

I = INITIATION

Punchline

Project INITIATION refers to the body of work completed to launch a project. This is your starting point.

Further Explanation

The goal of this group/phase is to document the scope[(G)] and purpose of the project at a relatively high level, and press play.

This process usually begins with a business case[(G)], where you look to determine whether or not the project is feasible, and ultimately, decide whether or not it is a go.

© 2019 | JD PALLAS Consulting | All Rights Reserved

II = PLANNING

Punchline

Project PLANNING refers to the body of work completed to:

- Establish the project scope
- Refine the project objectives
- Determine the project approach

Further Explanation

➢ **Scope** = summary of *exactly* what you want to accomplish

➢ **Objective** = aspirational purpose

➢ **Approach** = the course of action that will be taken to achieve all project goals

© 2019 | JD PALLAS Consulting | All Rights Reserved

III = EXECUTION

Punchline

Project EXECUTION refers to the process of completing the actual work required to satisfy the specific objectives of the project.

Further Explanation

For the project manager, this will typically require a fair amount of:

1. **Facilitation** – coordinating all project team members who are individually and collectively responsible for doing the work

2. **Diligence** – continuously following up with all team members until everything gets done

© 2019 | JD PALLAS Consulting | All Rights Reserved

IV = MONITORING & CONTROL

Punchline

Project MONITORING & CONTROL refers to the process of tracking, reviewing, and managing project progress and performance.

Further Explanation

You know the schedule, you know the scope of work, and you know the budget. How well are you tracking against your estimates and requirements? This is where metrics and reporting come into play.

Note – There is a *point of diminishing returns*[G] in this process group. Be careful not to over- nor under-engineer your approach here.

V = CLOSEOUT

Punchline

Project CLOSEOUT refers to the act of finalizing all activities across each of the process groups, in order to formally end the project.

Further Explanation

Follow through to the (actual) finish!

Make sure you don't leave any loose ends because they can definitely and often times will come back to haunt you.

It's not done until it's ALL done.

© 2019 | JD PALLAS Consulting | All Rights Reserved   26

TOOLKIT

PLAN

what all needs to get done?

TEXTBOOK TALK

According to the Project Management Body of Knowledge (PMBOK), a *project plan* is "a formal, approved document used to guide both project execution and project control."

"The primary uses of the project plan are to document planning assumptions and decisions, facilitate communication among project stakeholders[(G)], and document approved scope, cost, and schedule baselines. A project plan may be summarized or detailed."

I	II	III	IV	V

© 2019 | JD PALLAS Consulting | All Rights Reserved

SIMPLE BREAKDOWN

A project plan is not much more than a very detailed to-do list. Here's what makes it different from your average pen & paper to-do list:

1. **ALL project task details are organized by category.**

   Most project plans capture all of the following points of critical information, for each individual project task:
   - What = Task Description
   - Who = Owner/Resource
   - When = Start & Finish Date
   - Where = Workstream/Function

© 2019 | JD PALLAS Consulting | All Rights Reserved

31

SIMPLE BREAKDOWN (continued)

A project plan is not much more than a very detailed to-do list. Here's what makes it different from your average pen & paper to-do list:

2. **Milestones**(G) **highlight the project's critical path to completion.**

   By grouping related and/or sequential tasks together under individual milestones, stakeholders can easily follow the consecutive series of steps that must be taken, in order to get from point *A* to point *B*.

© 2019 | JD PALLAS Consulting | All Rights Reserved

SIMPLE BREAKDOWN (continued)

A project plan is not much more than a very detailed to-do list. Here's what makes it different from your average pen & paper to-do list:

3. **Dependencies between tasks can easily be captured and demonstrated.**

   Some tasks can be executed in parallel, whereas others cannot begin until certain tasks before them have been completed. These interconnections are called *task dependencies*(G).

I	II	III	IV	V

© 2019 | JD PALLAS Consulting | All Rights Reserved

BASIC BENEFITS

Your project plan is the one place in which all project task information should be stored and *continuously* updated. Doing so ensures the following:

- **The entire project team is on the same page** (everyone knows exactly what's supposed to be done, when, why, how, and by whom).

- It is **easy to identify and address bottlenecks**[(G)].

- It is **easy to develop status reports**.

ILLUSTRATION & TEMPLATE LINK

www.littlepmtoolkit.com/plan

© 2019 | JD PALLAS Consulting | All Rights Reserved

ID	Task Name	Phase	Workstream	Resource	Start	Baseline	Finish	Actual	% Complete	Milestone	Notes
1	PROJECT TITLE	ALL	ALL	ALL	1/2/18	7/17/18	7/17/18	N/A	90%	ALL	
2	INITIATION	Initiation	PMO	J. Pallas	1/2/18	2/1/18	2/1/18	2/3/18	100%	Initiation Milestone 1	
3	Initiation Milestone 1	Initiation	PMO	J. Pallas	1/2/18	1/9/18	1/9/18	2/1/18	100%	Initiation Milestone 1	
4	Initiation Milestone 1 - Project Task 1	Initiation	PMO	J. Pallas	1/2/18	1/9/18	1/9/18	2/1/18	100%	Initiation Milestone 1	
5	Initiation Milestone 1 - Project Task 2	Initiation	PMO	J. Pallas	1/2/18	1/9/18	1/9/18	2/1/18	100%	Initiation Milestone 1	
6	Initiation Milestone 1 - Project Task 3	Initiation	PMO	J. Pallas	1/2/18	1/9/18	1/9/18	2/1/18	100%	Initiation Milestone 1	
7	Initiation Milestone 2	Initiation	PMO	J. Pallas	1/9/18	1/23/18	1/23/18	1/23/18	100%	Initiation Milestone 2	
8	Initiation Milestone 2 - Project Task 1	Initiation	PMO	J. Pallas	1/9/18	1/10/18	1/10/18	1/10/18	100%	Initiation Milestone 2	
9	Initiation Milestone 2 - Project Task 2	Initiation	PMO	J. Pallas	1/10/18	1/17/18	1/17/18	1/17/18	100%	Initiation Milestone 2	Xyz...
10	Initiation Milestone 2 - Project Task 3	Initiation	PMO	J. Pallas	1/17/18	1/23/18	1/23/18	1/23/18	100%	Initiation Milestone 2	
11	Initiation Milestone 3	Initiation	PMO	J. Pallas	1/23/18	2/1/18	2/1/18	2/1/18	100%	Initiation Milestone 3	
12	Initiation Milestone 3 - Project Task 1	Initiation	PMO	J. Pallas	1/23/18	2/1/18	2/1/18	2/1/18	100%	Initiation Milestone 3	
13	Initiation Milestone 3 - Project Task 2	Initiation	PMO	J. Pallas	1/23/18	2/1/18	2/1/18	2/1/18	100%	Initiation Milestone 3	
14	Initiation Milestone 3 - Project Task 3	Initiation	PMO	J. Pallas	1/23/18	2/1/18	2/1/18	2/1/18	100%	Initiation Milestone 3	
15	PLANNING	Planning	PMO	J. Pallas	2/1/18	2/15/18	2/15/18	2/15/18	100%	Planning	
16	Planning Project Task 1	Planning	HR	O. Gerard	2/1/18	2/15/18	2/15/18	2/15/18	100%	Planning	
17	Planning Project Task 2	Planning	Marketing	J. Dunn	2/1/18	2/15/18	2/15/18	2/15/18	100%	Planning	
18	Planning Project Task 3	Planning	IT	M. Williams	2/1/18	2/15/18	2/15/18	2/15/18	100%	Planning	
19	Planning Project Task 4	Planning	Compliance	J. Name	2/1/18	2/15/18	2/15/18	2/15/18	100%	Planning	
20	Planning Project Task 5	Planning	Operations	A. Rothkopf	2/1/18	2/15/18	2/15/18	2/15/18	100%	Planning	
21	Planning Project Task 6	Planning	Finance	K. Hubbard	2/1/18	2/15/18	2/15/18	2/15/18	100%	Planning	
22	EXECUTION	Execution	ALL	J. Pallas	2/15/18	6/18/18	6/18/18	N/A	95%	Execution Milestone 1	
23	Execution Milestone 1	Execution	IT	M. Williams	2/15/18	4/19/18	4/19/18	4/19/18	100%	Execution Milestone 1	
24	Execution Milestone 1 - Project Task 1	Execution	IT	M. Williams	2/15/18	3/15/18	3/15/18	3/15/18	100%	Execution Milestone 1	
25	Execution Milestone 1 - Project Task 2	Execution	IT	M. Williams	3/16/18	3/23/18	3/23/18	3/23/18	100%	Execution Milestone 1	Abc...
26	Execution Milestone 1 - Project Task 3	Execution	IT	M. Williams	3/16/18	3/30/18	3/30/18	3/30/18	100%	Execution Milestone 1	
27	Execution Milestone 1 - Project Task 4	Execution	IT	M. Williams	3/16/18	3/30/18	3/30/18	3/30/18	100%	Execution Milestone 1	
28	Execution Milestone 1 - Project Task 5	Execution	IT	M. Williams	4/2/18	4/19/18	4/19/18	4/19/18	100%	Execution Milestone 1	
29	Execution Milestone 2	Execution	Operations	A. Rothkopf	2/15/18	5/15/18	5/15/18	5/15/18	100%	Execution Milestone 2	
30	Execution Milestone 2 - Project Task 1	Execution	Operations	A. Rothkopf	2/15/18	2/19/18	2/19/18	2/19/18	100%	Execution Milestone 2	

© 2019 | JD PALLAS Consulting | All Rights Reserved

BEST PRACTICES

✓ **There should be one document owner. Period.** The project manager is typically the single party responsible for the development, update, accuracy, and completeness of this document, from start to finish.

✓ **Use MS Project, MS Excel, or an alternative software tool** to develop this document. These and other grid-based applications will make life MUCH easier when you are creating your project plan.

I	II	III	IV	V

© 2019 | JD PALLAS Consulting | All Rights Reserved

BEST PRACTICES (continued)

✓ **Use your columns.** Using individual columns to identify relevant categories of information can help you target the assessment of both progress and bottlenecks.

➤ Task Description(G)
➤ Owner(G)/Resource(G)
➤ Function(G)/Department(G)
➤ Workstream(G)
➤ Project Phase(G)
➤ Milestone(G)
➤ Dates(G): Start, Finish, Baseline, Actual
➤ Percent Complete(G)
➤ Notes(G)

BEST PRACTICES (continued)

✓ **Describe each task thoroughly.** Make sure a complete outsider could (theoretically) understand each individual line item.

✓ **Distinguish between planned and actual finish dates.** This is critical for project performance measurement. Simple line graphs derived from these data points clearly indicate how well your project team is tracking against its project schedule.

I	II	III	IV	V

BEST PRACTICES (continued)

✓ **Delineate your project milestones, and group your tasks accordingly.** Clearly indicating specific project "mile markers" helps stakeholders to immediately understand "where you are" at any given moment.

✓ **Set your baseline and never change it.** Before execution begins, establish the estimated start and finish dates for each individual task with its respective owner, and lock down that prefixed timeline as the project baseline.

BEST PRACTICES (continued)

✓ **Obtain progress updates, regularly**. Team members should expect to receive a request for updates (regarding all open tasks that are set to come due) on the preset day of your working cycle, like clockwork – as indicated in the PM [project management] protocol.

✓ **NEVER delete/override project plan files.** Always save the latest version of this document with the current date called out in the file name. You never know what you may need to go back and reference.

| I | II | III | IV | V |

BEST PRACTICES (continued)

✓ **Make it public** (to all project team members). In the interest of full transparency, you should always publish the most recent version of the project plan, every time you have made any major, bulk, or otherwise material update.

PROTOCOL

how will we get it done?

TEXTBOOK TALK

The *project management (PM) protocol* is not a tool you will find explicitly captured in the PMBOK Guide; however, it is definitely a critical success factor.

It refers to the system of rules or the official procedure that ultimately governs all project management processes and activity throughout the duration of the project. The most important fixture of this tool is the establishment of the precise cadence[(G)] for all project management activity.

SIMPLE BREAKDOWN

This tool is basically a **miniature process flow document or illustration**, focused exclusively on project management activity and resource interactions.

It is extremely important that everyone on the project team is immediately and collectively operating under a single set of expectations and conditions.

So, from the very beginning, you need **to tell the project team exactly what you are going to do *and* how you are going to do it.**

© 2019 | JD PALLAS Consulting | All Rights Reserved

BASIC BENEFITS

The absence of a pre-established protocol can lead to a severe lack of productivity and overall project execution efficiency.

As such, this is the one document in which the sequence of all recurring project management events should be illustrated and distributed, thus providing the following:

- Formal/informal commitment to the system of project delivery

- Expectation setting and leveling, with regards to team member participation/involvement

© 2019 | JD PALLAS Consulting | All Rights Reserved

ILLUSTRATION & TEMPLATE LINK

www.littlepmtoolkit.com/protocol

© 2019 | JD PALLAS Consulting | All Rights Reserved

PROJECT MANAGEMENT PROTOCOL

	WEEK 1	WEEK 2
MONDAY	Project Task Execution Continues To Be Executed According To Project Plan & Issues / Action Log Schedule	• Project Plan / Task Progress Update Returned By All Relevant Project Team Members • Project Plan Updated (PM) • Status Report Created (PM) • Project Task Execution Continues...
TUESDAY	Project Task Execution Continues To Be Executed According To Project Plan & Issues / Action Log Schedule	• Meeting Agenda Distributed To The Project Team • Status Report Distributed To The Project Team • Project Task Execution Continues...
WEDNESDAY	Project Task Execution Continues To Be Executed According To Project Plan & Issues / Action Log Schedule	• *** BI-WEEKLY STATUS MEETING *** • Project Task Execution Continues...
THURSDAY	• Project Plan / Task Progress Update Requests Submitted to All Relevant Project Team Members (% Complete, Issues, Risks, Bottlenecks, & Changes) • Project Task Execution Continues...	• Meeting Minutes Published • Project Task Execution Continues...
FRIDAY	Project Task Execution Continues To Be Executed According To Project Plan & Issues / Action Log Schedule	Project Task Execution Continues To Be Executed According To Project Plan & Issues / Action Log Schedule

www.jdpallasconsulting.com

770.568.6961
info@jdpallas.com

© 2019 | JD PALLAS Consulting | All Rights Reserved

BEST PRACTICES

✓ **Make it an infographic**(G). In general, whenever you need to explain a cyclical process of any kind, an image will be easier to recall than a block of text.

✓ **Obtain confirmation from everyone involved.** Whether latent or direct, ensure that all relevant stakeholders have seen and agree to the protocol that you are looking to establish for the execution of all project management activities.

| I | II | III | IV | V |

© 2019 | JD PALLAS Consulting | All Rights Reserved

BEST PRACTICES (continued)

✓ **Be consistent. Don't waver.** Since *you* are facilitating all of the activity referenced in the protocol, it is critical that you deliver on the "promise" of what you have established.

✓ **Be reasonable.** IF there is a legitimate reason to tweak the protocol at some point, it's fine (i.e., shifting from a weekly to a bi-weekly cycle because the project is performing well and team members now require fewer touch points).

I	II	III	IV	V

© 2019 | JD PALLAS Consulting | All Rights Reserved

REPORTING

where are we right now?

TEXTBOOK TALK

The *project status report* is a regular, formalized report on project progress that is measured against the schedule of deliverables captured in the project plan.

The purpose of this tool is to communicate a project's status effectively and efficiently to all relevant project stakeholders.

The project status report is the single tool in which all progress communication and issue escalation should be centralized.

SIMPLE BREAKDOWN

This tool is essentially **a snapshot of the project's current state**, illustrating each of the following pieces of key information:

1. Where the project stands as of the date on which the report was generated

2. Why it stands there and how it got there

3. How it intends to and what all it needs to get or remain on track

© 2019 | JD PALLAS Consulting | All Rights Reserved

SIMPLE BREAKDOWN (continued)

Commonly, this document houses a few main components, on a single PowerPoint slide, as follows:

- **Document ID information** – project title, report date, company name, etc.

- **Overall red/amber/green (RAG) status**[(G)] – current and previous and/or projected

- **Executive summary** – a brief but comprehensive synopsis of the project's current state, capturing the most critical updates

SIMPLE BREAKDOWN (continued)

Commonly, this document houses a few main components, on a single PowerPoint slide, as follows:

- **Critical or high priority issues & risks** – callout of bottlenecks/ potential bottlenecks, requiring immediate/continuous attention

- **Workstream/Resource specific RAG status** – individual status indicators, broken down by relevant subgroup

- **Additional options** – triple constraint[G] RAGs, planned vs. actual graph

© 2019 | JD PALLAS Consulting | All Rights Reserved

BASIC BENEFITS

The status report is the one standard document in which all official project updates should be captured. This is crucial, because:

- *When done properly*, it provides **an objective assessment** on the overall health of the project.

- It **makes sure the entire project team is on the same page.** (Everyone knows exactly what has been done or not done – when, why, how, and by whom.)

- It directly **calls out all noteworthy issues, risks, and bottlenecks.**

BASIC BENEFITS (continued)

Rule of Thumb

Depending on how and when your status reports are generated, you may have the option to distribute them to your stakeholders either before or after each status meeting.

When possible, it is ALWAYS better to **distribute your project status report PRIOR to each status meeting**. Reason being, you can collectively discuss how to push things forward, from a single reference point (based on the updates captured).

ILLUSTRATION & TEMPLATE LINK

www.littlepmtoolkit.com/reporting

© 2019 | JD PALLAS Consulting | All Rights Reserved

[PROJECT NAME] : STATUS REPORT

EXECUTIVE SUMMARY

- **BULLET TOPIC #1 :** Bullet Summary...
- **BULLET TOPIC #2 :**
  - Bullet Summary...
  - Bullet Summary...
- **BULLET TOPIC #3 :** Bullet Summary...
- **BULLET TOPIC #4 :** Bullet Summary...

OVERALL PROGRESS

previous	current	projected
A	G	G

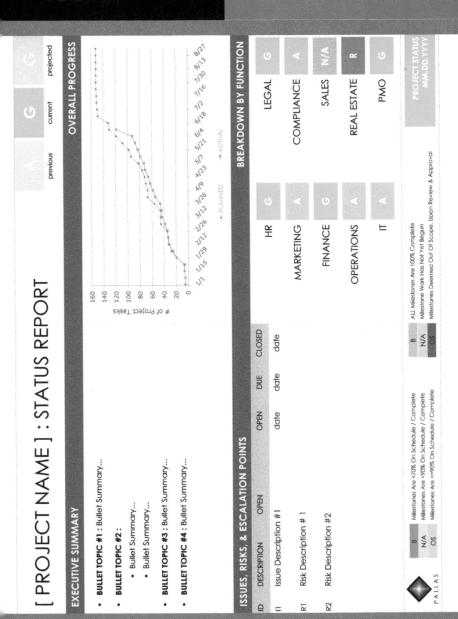

# of Project Tasks (160, 140, 120, 100, 80, 60, 40, 20, 0)

1/1, 1/15, 1/29, 2/12, 2/26, 3/12, 3/26, 4/9, 4/23, 5/7, 5/21, 6/4, 6/18, 7/2, 7/16, 7/30, 8/13, 8/27

PLANNED   ACTUAL

ISSUES, RISKS, & ESCALATION POINTS

ID	DESCRIPTION	OPEN	OPEN	DUE	CLOSED
			date	date	date
I1	Issue Description #1				
R1	Risk Description #1				
R2	Risk Description #2				

BREAKDOWN BY FUNCTION

HR	G	LEGAL	G
MARKETING	A	COMPLIANCE	A
FINANCE	G	SALES	N/A
OPERATIONS	A	REAL ESTATE	R
IT	A	PMO	G

B	Milestones Are <70% On Schedule / Complete
N/A	Milestones Are <90% On Schedule / Complete
OS	Milestones Are >=90% On Schedule / Complete

B	ALL Milestones Are 100% Complete
N/A	Milestone Work Has Not Yet Begun
OS	Milestones Deemed Out Of Scope, Upon Review & Approval

PROJECT STATUS
MM.DD.YYYY

PALLAS

© 2019 | JD PALLAS Consulting | All Rights Reserved

59

BEST PRACTICES

✓ **The BEST status reports consistently combine and illustrate objective performance measurement with subjective expert interpretation.**

✓ **Keep to one single format.** Try to use a single PowerPoint-esque document template for your status report, throughout the duration of the project.

✓ **Use bullets.** No one wants to read a project status *novel*. Ever.

I	II	III	IV	V

© 2019 | JD PALLAS Consulting | All Rights Reserved   60

BEST PRACTICES (continued)

✓ **Less is more.** If possible, try to contain your status report to one slide – highlighting only the most important points of information that will be generally useful to stakeholders, across the board.

✓ **Use negative space.** A status report that is too densely packed with information may be exhausting to stakeholders, who will in turn not take in all of the information you are trying to communicate.

I	II	III	IV	V

BEST PRACTICES (continued)

✓ **Infographics are great.** Pictures are often more quickly and better understood than words (i.e., progress graph, Gantt Chart, measurement snapshots, etc.)

✓ **Best practice status report quadrants:**

➢ EXECUTIVE SUMMARY (subjective assessment)

➢ OVERALL PROGRESS (objective measurement)

➢ KEY ISSUES & RISKS (subjective assessment)

➢ PROGRESS BREAKDOWN (objective measurement)

AGENDA

what do we need to discuss?

TEXTBOOK TALK

A *meeting agenda* is a list of discussion topics or activities, sequenced in the order in which they are to be taken up. They typically begin with an introduction or roll call and end with an action item recap, final questions, and adjournment.

Agendas usually call out one or more specific items of business that must be collectively acted upon, in the immediate term.

SIMPLE BREAKDOWN

A meeting agenda is simply a **discussion overview and outline** that preemptively answers the following questions for all meeting attendees:

1. What is the overall purpose of this meeting?

2. Who all was invited to this meeting?

3. What are we going to talk about/do, during this meeting?

4. How long is each segment expected to last?

BASIC BENEFITS

The main benefit of this tool is that it targets the focus of each stakeholder on the status of project activity that is currently underway.

Additionally, it allows stakeholders to prepare in advance with noteworthy updates, open questions, escalation points, etc.

And lastly, agendas serve as a prefixed guide to help the meeting facilitator ensure that the meeting discussion remains on track (regarding both time and subject matter).

ILLUSTRATION & TEMPLATE LINK

www.littlepmtoolkit.com/agenda

© 2019 | JD PALLAS Consulting | All Rights Reserved

PALLAS

[PROJECT NAME]

MEETING AGENDA

PARTICIPANTS

ORGANIZER : Jackson Pallas (PM)

INVITEES : James Cooney (ES), Lucy Propper (BO), Leticia Jaimes, Brandon Scott, Richard Hale, Antoine Carter, Rachel Moore, David Dillard, Matthew Helem, Amanda Gergi, Lindsay Mar, Nicholas McDonald, Edwin Dixon, Scotti Mags

DISCUSSION TOPICS

ROLL CALL	~ 2 min
OPEN ACTION ITEMS	~ 5 min
STATUS REPORT REVIEW	~ 10 min
WORKSTREAM / FUNCTION UPDATES	~ 40 min
1. Operations	~ 10 min
2. Finance	~ 10 min
3. Compliance	~ 10 min
4. IT	~ 10 min
OPEN FORUM	
ADJOURNMENT	

www.jdpallasconsulting.com

770.568.6961
info@jdpallas.com

© 2019 | JD PALLAS Consulting | All Rights Reserved

68

BEST PRACTICES

✓ **Email is OK.** Presuming the project is not *extremely* formal (according to you as the project manager and/ or the powers that be), it's perfectly fine to draft the meeting agenda in the body of a meeting invite email.

✓ **Otherwise, use a template.** IF it is *not* included in the body of the meeting invite email, try to consistently use a single document format for the meeting agenda.

| I | II | III | IV | V |

© 2019 | JD PALLAS Consulting | All Rights Reserved

BEST PRACTICES (continued)

✓ **Prioritize discussion topics.** You should always sequence your discussion points in order of importance.

✓ **Preset estimated discussion times for each topic.** Always try to indicate how much time should be dedicated to each discussion segment.

✓ **Use your status report.** It is great form to use the contents of your status report to frame your agenda points, when possible.

BEST PRACTICES (continued)

✓ **Distribute in advance.** Always *try* to distribute the agenda to invitees at least 24 hours before the meeting – allowing an opportunity for key stakeholders to weigh in, if need be.

✓ **Call out the speakers.** When your meeting is expected to have different speakers/facilitators for each segment, be sure to identify them, accordingly, in the agenda.

| I | II | III | IV | V |

© 2019 | JD PALLAS Consulting | All Rights Reserved

71

MEETING

let's talk about where we are now and what still needs to get done.

TEXTBOOK TALK

Status meetings are regularly scheduled events for stakeholders to provide updates and exchange information about the project.

The **cadence** of your status meeting schedule **should be fixed**, meaning the frequency and duration of your scheduled status meetings should be established up front and adhered to throughout.

The two most common types of status meetings are (1) working group, and (2) steering group.

© 2019 | JD PALLAS Consulting | All Rights Reserved

TEXTBOOK TALK (continued)

Working Group Meeting

This forum gathers your **core team of project stakeholders**, to discuss the progress, issues, and risks surrounding the execution of the project tasks, in order to do the following:

1. Track all completed and in-progress deliverables that have been scheduled for completion by that point

2. Raise/escalate any potential bottlenecks that are currently hindering progress

TEXTBOOK TALK (continued)

Steering Group Meeting

This forum gathers your **senior team of project sponsors and executive advisors**, to discuss the progress, issues, and risks surrounding the achievement of project milestones, in order to do the following:

1. Ensure continued strategic alignment between business strategy and project scope

2. Clear any potential bottlenecks that are currently hindering progress

© 2019 | JD PALLAS Consulting | All Rights Reserved   76

SIMPLE BREAKDOWN

First off, **yes, a meeting is a tool.**

Think of this tool as your project's "mile markers." Recurring meetings are continuously and consistently fixed points on the project path that inform all relevant stakeholders how the project team is performing (both collectively and individually), in relation to what needs to have been done by that point in time.

This tool is one of the best ways to keep your project team both focused and forthright.

SIMPLE BREAKDOWN (continued)

Consider this: If you were to have a meeting with your teammates every week to talk about what has been done, what should be done, and what needs to get done, it would be virtually impossible to hide from your individual responsibilities in the overall matter. Right?

Generally speaking, **NO ONE wants to be called out for not doing something they were supposed to do**, especially when other people are depending on it.

SIMPLE BREAKDOWN (continued)

Additional Point of Note:

Status meetings are **not** the same as topical/ad hoc meetings.

Ad hoc meetings are held on a one-off basis, at various points throughout the life of the project with *specific* intent for *specific* team members to update, discuss, and/or produce *specific* project tasks/deliverables during the meeting itself.

BASIC BENEFITS

The most significant benefit of a status meeting is that all relevant stakeholders can be simultaneously and collectively apprised of and/or talk through each of the following, in order to **make sure everyone is on the exact same page:**

- Overall progress
- Issues, bottlenecks, and risks
- Callouts/escalation points
- Cross-functional dependencies
- Immediate next steps

ILLUSTRATION & TEMPLATE LINK

www.littlepmtoolkit.com/meeting

© 2019 | JD PALLAS Consulting | All Rights Reserved

MEETING CADENCE OPTIONS

INTERNAL STAKEHOLDERS

Core Project Team
- Weekly
- Bi-weekly
- Monthly

Working Group
- Weekly
- Bi-weekly
- Monthly

Steering Committee
- Monthly
- Quarterly
- Semi-annually

EXTERNAL STAKEHOLDERS

Clients
- Weekly
- Bi-weekly
- Monthly

Vendors
- Weekly
- Bi-weekly

General Public
- Quarterly
- Semi-annually
- Annually

© 2019 | JD PALLAS Consulting | All Rights Reserved

82

BEST PRACTICES

✓ **Do NOT meet just for the sake of meeting.** If there is no pressing business to discuss, it's okay to cancel (where possible, at least a few hours in advance).

✓ **Longer does not automatically mean better.** There is no need to hold a two-hour meeting for what clearly only warrants a 30-45 minute discussion.

✓ **Conference calls are great for regular, "unsurprising" updates. And, in-person meetings are ALWAYS best for true group discussion.**

I	II	III	IV	V

BEST PRACTICES (continued)

✓ **Let people know in advance if they will be expected to speak.**

✓ **Roll call.** ALWAYS begin the meeting by identifying/ confirming who is in the meeting (when reasonable, i.e., not more than ~30 attendees).

✓ **Begin with the elephants in the room.** Open your meetings by addressing any urgent/pressing items that remain outstanding since the previous meeting (especially if they might impact the current meeting discussion).

I	II	III	IV	V

© 2019 | JD PALLAS Consulting | All Rights Reserved

BEST PRACTICES (continued)

✓ **Follow your agenda.** You made and shared it for a reason.

✓ **Stick to the schedule.** Try to keep to the time allotted for each topic, as indicated in your meeting agenda.
  ➤ Note: It is okay to *occasionally* veer off the agenda schedule (for a valid reason like a newly discovered issue).

✓ **Use your status report.** It is (also) a great idea to use your status report as a tool to guide the meeting discussion.

© 2019 | JD PALLAS Consulting | All Rights Reserved

BEST PRACTICES (continued)

✓ **Recap the big stuff.** End each meeting with a recap of the outstanding/new action items, to ensure that everyone knows exactly what's supposed to be done, and why, and how, and by when and by whom.

✓ **Allow space for questions.** If possible – after the main agenda items have been covered – open up the floor for attendees to present any inquiries/concerns they may have to fellow project team members.

I	II	III	IV	V

© 2019 | JD PALLAS Consulting | All Rights Reserved

MINUTES

what did we discuss & decide?

TEXTBOOK TALK

Meeting minutes are written or otherwise recorded documentation that is used to inform attendees and non-attendees about what was discussed/what happened throughout the course of a meeting.

These notes are generally taken or recorded during the meeting itself so participants can have a real-time record of the event.

SIMPLE BREAKDOWN

Simply put, these are **official meeting notes** that capture the most important points of the discussion, in as little or as much detail as necessary (based on the overall complexity of the project).

Basically, meeting minutes formally document the following:

a) **Who was there**
b) **What was discussed**
c) **What the next steps are**

Most commonly, this tool is formatted/organized into the following buckets…

© 2019 | JD PALLAS Consulting | All Rights Reserved

SIMPLE BREAKDOWN (continued)

- All meeting attendee names

- Notes regarding the agenda topics that were covered

- Any key decisions that were made by the attendees during the meeting

- All follow-up actions items that were committed to by any given attendee, and their respective due dates for completion

- Any other noteworthy events or points worth documenting for future reference

| I | II | III | IV | V |

© 2019 | JD PALLAS Consulting | All Rights Reserved

BASIC BENEFITS

Anyone who has ever managed any group project can attest to it being extremely beneficial to have a single, centralized record of working discussions that were held, in order to:

1. Reference when executing future project work

2. Leverage as business case support when escalating any potential issues and/or defending subsequent activity

3. Verify decisions and track commitments that were made, during any given meeting

© 2019 | JD PALLAS Consulting | All Rights Reserved

ILLUSTRATION & TEMPLATE LINK

www.littlepmtoolkit.com/minutes

© 2019 | JD PALLAS Consulting | All Rights Reserved

[PROJECT NAME]

Month DD, YYYY > 9:30am-10:30am

MEETING MINUTES

PARTICIPANTS

ORGANIZER : Jackson Pallas (PM)

ATTENDEES : Lucy Propper (BO), Leticia Jaimes, Brandon Scott, Richard Hale.
Antoine Carter, Rachel Moore, David Dillard, Matthew Helem, Amanda
Gergi, Nicholas McDonald, Jane Few

DISCUSSION POINTS

OPEN / NEW ACTION ITEMS
- None at present

OVERALL STATUS
- The overall project is currently on track to meet our 12/31 deadline.
- The delinquency issue raised in our last meeting have been escalated
  through the appropriate channels and are on schedule for resolution by
  the end of this week. The Business Owner (BO) will update the team
  once the issue has officially been closed.

WORKSTREAM / FUNCTION UPDATES

OPERATIONS
- The Operations team has completed yadda yadda and has now
  moved onto X, Y, and Z.
- Ops has a critical dependency on IT to deliver the wigwag before they
  can move forward with that thingamabob.
- ......

© 2019 | JD PALLAS Consulting | All Rights Reserved

93

BEST PRACTICES

✓ **Make it official.** ONLY produce this document on an official company letterhead/template.

➤ NEVER type them inside the body of an email

✓ **Use one consistent header.** Capture all basic project information at the top of the document (as relevant):

➤ Company
➤ (Project managing) department
➤ Project title
➤ Meeting title
➤ Date
➤ (Confirmed/actual) attendees

BEST PRACTICES (continued)

✓ **Use one template, throughout.** Try to establish and consistently use a single document format for the meeting minutes. (i.e., create a template that works and stick with it).

✓ **Leverage your agenda.** Use the meeting agenda topics to format/outline the discussion points captured in the meeting minutes.

I	II	III	IV	V

© 2019 | JD PALLAS Consulting | All Rights Reserved

BEST PRACTICES (continued)

✓ **Highlight the important stuff.** Be sure to call out any of the following that were identified or confirmed during the meeting:

➤ Key decisions

➤ Project issues/bottlenecks

➤ Newly identified project risks

➤ Other relevant escalation points (for management to address)

➤ Immediate-term action items (Note: An action item is not the same as a project task – which should always be captured in the project plan.)

© 2019 | JD PALLAS Consulting | All Rights Reserved

BEST PRACTICES (continued)

✓ **Don't overdo it.** Only capture as much *verbatim* discussion as necessary. (Don't overkill it if you don't have to.)

➤ When this is necessary, be sure to identify (in shorthand if possible) which stakeholders said what.

✓ **Distribute the document to all meeting invitees within 24 hours of the meeting end time.**

✓ **Get feedback.** Allow 24 hours for corrections, additions, and/or clarification questions before the minutes are "sealed."

| I | II | III | IV | V |

BEST PRACTICES (continued)

✓ **Keep the minutes in a common, single storage location.** Store each document in a centralized repository (ideally accessible for viewing – NOT editing – by all project team members).

✓ **When possible, the minutes taker and the meeting facilitator should be different people.** Particularly for large teams or broader topical discussions, it is good practice for the facilitator **not** to be responsible for documenting the details of the discussion.

| I | II | III | IV | V |

© 2019 | JD PALLAS Consulting | All Rights Reserved

CONCLUSION

Remember each of the unknowing project managers referenced in the beginning of this book? Well, with the effective application of these six tools, **we will have resolved every single one of those pain points** (and then some).

Here's how this specific combination of tools (when used properly) often helps to mitigate the risk of each issue from even happening in the first place.

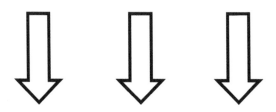

www.littlepmtoolkit.com/painpointschart

Bottom line, **you have just learned the** *meat and potatoes* **of what virtually every professional project manager has been using for years (in some way, shape, or form) to successfully deliver ALL of their team projects.**

At the end of the day, **project management is about keeping information and people both organized and on track.** Figure out what you've got to do, and then just get it done.

The six tools laid out in this guide will absolutely help you to get from point *A* to point *B* as efficiently and effectively as possible.

Furthermore, **the very best thing about this guidebook** is that each one of the aforementioned tools is:

1. **"Situation non-specific"** – meaning these tools can help any project manager be effective, regardless of variables like industry, subject matter, team member age, level of expertise, etc.

2. **Completely customizable** – meaning you can create and format these documents however you like, in order to accommodate/reflect your individual management style, team culture, etc. and still get the job done.

If you happen to have a team project set to begin right this moment, here's **exactly** what you need to do:

1. **PREPARE** – Create/download *standardized documentation templates* to use throughout the life of your project:

   - Meeting agenda (.doc)
   - Meeting minutes (.doc)
   - Project plan (.mpp or .xls)
   - Status report (.ppt or .xls)

2. **PLAN** – Talk to your team members and determine exactly what needs to get done (and how, and by when), given your overall project deadline.

© 2019 | JD PALLAS Consulting | All Rights Reserved

If you happen to have a team project set to begin right this moment, here's **exactly** what you need to do:

3. **ESTABLISH** – Set up your project management protocol (i.e., your daily, weekly, bi-weekly, monthly cycle of activity), and obtain confirmation/consensus from all team members.

4. **DO THE WORK** – Execute your project plan, managing the progress of all project activity as instructed throughout this text.

5. **CLOSE IT OUT** – Confirm that everything is done and move on to the next project.

Finally, to paraphrase the contents of this entire book into the simplest possible explanation…

In order to effectively and efficiently manage almost any team project, you simply need to do the following:

A. **Set it up.** By creating a project plan, establishing your project management protocol, and formulating a status report to use throughout.

- Project Plan
- PM Protocol
- **Status Report**

© 2019 | JD PALLAS Consulting | All Rights Reserved

Finally, to paraphrase the contents of this entire book into the simplest possible explanation…

In order to effectively and efficiently manage almost any team project, you simply need to do the following:

B. Knock it down. By following your protocol, obtaining regular progress updates on the tasks documented in your project plan, and facilitating regular status meetings to keep things on track.

- Meeting Agenda
- **Status Meeting**
- Meeting Minutes

© 2019 | JD PALLAS Consulting | All Rights Reserved

That's it. You are all set!!!

Right now, in this very moment, you are well-equipped to begin actively managing most project teams.

So…get to work.

© 2019 | JD PALLAS Consulting | All Rights Reserved

APPENDIX

- **actual finish date** – The confirmed date on which work for the associated project task has truly been completed.

- **baseline finish date** – The *original* estimated date on which work for the associated project task has been scheduled to conclude. This date should remain fixed, throughout the life of the project.

- **baseline start date** – The *original* estimated date on which work for the associated project task has been scheduled to begin. This date should remain fixed, throughout the life of the project.

- **bottleneck** – Any material delay or obstacle that prevents the completion of project tasks, or otherwise limits the working ability of project resources.

- **business case** – Justification for a proposed project on the basis of its expected economic benefit.

- **cadence** – The flow of events, especially referring to the pattern in which something is expected and experienced.

- **department** (a.k.a., function) – The working area that is ultimately responsible for the management and/or completion of a project task.

© 2019 | JD PALLAS Consulting | All Rights Reserved

- **finish date** – The estimated date by which work for the associated project task has been scheduled for completion.

- **function** (a.k.a., department) – The working area that is ultimately responsible for the management and/or completion of a project task.

- **infographic** – A visual image such as a chart or diagram used to represent information or data.

- **milestone** – An action or event marking a significant change or stage in project execution.

© 2019 | JD PALLAS Consulting | All Rights Reserved

- **notes** – Any additional, yet pertinent information regarding the associated project task.

- **owner** (a.k.a., resource) – The name of the specific individual or resource profile who is ultimately responsible for the management and completion of the associated task or milestone.

- **percent complete** – The (often estimated) percentage of work product that has actually been completed as the task owner moves toward marking the overall task as "complete" or "closed" (value may be set anywhere from 0% to 100%).

- **PMBOK** – Stands for Project Management Body of Knowledge and it is the entire collection of processes, best practices, terminologies, and guidelines that are accepted as standards within the project management industry.

- **PMI** – Stands for Project Management Institute and focuses on "delivering value for more than 2.9 million professionals working in nearly every country in the world through global collaboration, education and research." (source: pmi.org)

- **point of diminishing returns** – The point in a process where, when surpassed, as work effort continues to increase, the marginal value of that effort's output will begin to decrease.

- **process groups** – A standard grouping of work processes and product that collectively produce a single outcome.

- **project management** – The active, centralized management and coordination of progress towards a fixed end point or state, through finite, change-driven activity.

- **project phase** – The collection of the project tasks and activities that fall under a common work theme (i.e., *planning* work, *execution* work, etc.)

- **RAG status** – The colors of standard traffic lights (red, amber, green) used to signal a project's status, indicating how on track or at risk is the project is.

  ➢ **Green** indicates normal or on-track levels of progress.
  ➢ **Amber** indicates progress has slowed (or attention is otherwise warranted).
  ➢ **Red** indicates progress has stopped or is otherwise substantially delayed.

- **resource** (a.k.a., owner) – The name of the specific individual or resource profile who is ultimately responsible for the management and completion of the associated task or milestone.

- **scope** – The body of work that must be completed to deliver any product, service, or result with/to the agreed-upon specifications.

- **stakeholder** – An individual, group of individuals, or institution with any interest or concern in something, especially a business activity.

- **start date** – The estimated date on which work for the associated project task has been scheduled to begin.

- **task dependency** – the logical, preceding relationship between two project activities, or between a project activity and a project milestone.

- **task description** – Summary detail that generally explains the work task, effort, product, and/or deliverable that must be completed.

- **triple constraint** – Combination of the three most significant restrictions for any project: time, cost, and scope.

- **workstream** – Any area or activity grouping into which project activity may be divided.

© 2019 | JD PALLAS Consulting | All Rights Reserved

To book the author for speaking engagements, employee training, continuing education, or executive coaching, you may submit your request via email or telephone at:

info@jacksonpallas.com
1.917.983.7933

For additional information about product licensing, the author, or project management, please visit:

www.littlepmtoolkit.com
www.jacksonpallas.com
www.pmosetup.com

ABOUT THE AUTHOR

Co-founder & CEO of JD PALLAS Consulting, **Jackson Pallas** provides extraordinary solutions for organizations – of all sizes, across all industries – with enhancement opportunities and transformation requirements involving the following:

❖ Corporate & business strategy
❖ Program & project management
❖ Process improvement
❖ Change management
❖ Brand development

For more information, please visit:
www.jdpallasconsulting.com
www.jacksonpallas.com
@jacksonpallas 🐦 📷 in f

© 2019 | JD PALLAS Consulting | All Rights Reserved

An astounding **97% of organizations** believe project management is critical to business performance and organizational success. (source: PwC)

For every $1 billion invested in the United States, **$122 million was wasted** due to lacking project performance. (source: pmi.org)

That's absolutely ridiculous. So, I wrote this pocket guide in an effort to help ALL Project Managers, on ANY TYPE of project team, strip away the unnecessary distractions commonly found in most how-to literature, and just…simply…
#GETITDONE

© 2019 | JD PALLAS Consulting | All Rights Reserved

CPSIA information can be obtained
at www.ICGtesting.com
Printed in the USA
LVHW010821041119
636240LV00006B/281/P